SO YOU CAN'T FORGIVE?

To Paula,

I hope this helps to unlock the door to Freedom and Peace. N. xx

2-8-14

Brian Lennon SJ

So You Can't Forgive?
MOVING TOWARDS FREEDOM

the columba press

First published in 2009 by
the columba press
55A Spruce Avenue, Stillorgan Industrial Park,
Blackrock, Co Dublin

Origination by The Columba Press
Printed in Ireland by ColourBooks Ltd, Dublin

ISBN 978-1-85607-637-1

Note:

The names and circumstances of stories in this book which are not in the public arena have been changed so that they bear no similarity to any living person.

Table of Contents

PART ONE

Separating ourselves from wrongdoers

Introduction

In 2008 Josef Fritzl was arrested in Austria for imprisoning his daughter for 24 years, raping her continuously during that period, fathering seven children by her, and keeping them imprisoned.

Should we forgive Fritzl? Should his daughter forgive him? Most people I know would answer an emphatic 'No' to that question. Nor would they expect his daughter to forgive him. But they might expect people in other situations to forgive – for example, a woman whose husband had been killed by a drunk driver, or someone who has lost a loved one in conflict. In Northern Ireland people often say that 'forgiveness' is the only way forward.

This means that people whose loved ones have been murdered, or who have lost people to drunk drivers, and others, can have a different expectation put on them by society than that put on the daughter of Josef Fritzl. There is no pressure on her to forgive. Quite the opposite. But in these other situations, while people may not be told to their face that they should forgive, they will hear general calls for them to do so. If they do not respond some people will say: 'They're stuck. They never got over it. They were not able to let it go.' And maybe this will be true.

If they are Christians they will hear sermons in church talking about how Our Lord forgave those who wronged him and how he calls us to do the same.

So a different burden is put on some people.

A friend of mine who works as a counsellor had a client who was a devout Christian. She had been abused by her father when she was a child. She hated him as a result. She could not forgive him. She felt deeply angry. But what made things worse for her was that as a Christian she felt she should be able to forgive and in her adult life be able to have a new relationship with her father, to let the past rest. Because she could not do this, she felt huge guilt and that she was failing to respond to the call of God and to her church teaching. She stopped practising her religion and then felt a double failure. Her understanding of what the scriptures say about forgiving added to her trauma.

My friend remarked that something similar happened with many of his clients who were open to a Christian faith, but far less to those who were not.

People with Christian faith may suffer in a number of ways: first they have their pain; then their anger; then they think others see them in a poor light because they cannot forgive. On top of that they can see themselves as bad in the eyes of God and of their church. It is worth unpacking forgiving, if only to see if the burden we put on some people is justified.

If you ask people why they would not forgive, the answer that many give suggests that they fear doing so would involve some element of excusing, minimising or justifying the wrong that has been done; or else they think it means letting the wrongdoer off punishment.

In my view these ideas about what forgiving means are incorrect. The meaning of forgiving is one issue which will come up in the pages that follow.

My focus in this book is on people as individuals, not as members of groups. Individuals are part of society and as part of society they play a role in the groups to which they belong. Further things need therefore to be said about group forgiving, responsibility and repenting.

Secondly, my focus is on those who have suffered wrong. Other things need to be said about wrongdoers and what they need to do. But here I am going to focus on individuals who have been hurt.

The ideas in this book have come to me from many sources. One is my work for nearly 30 years with people suffering in the Northern Ireland conflict. That conflict left many broken hearts and bodies. The bereaved face a chair that will always be empty. Some have been able to move towards freedom, some have not.

A second source is counselling: I have been privileged to walk with people who struggled with difficulties in their lives; I have learnt much from conversations I have had with others who did similar work; and I have gleaned bits of insight from my own journey.

The third source is from spirituality and theology: again looking at my own and others' journeys, and trying to understand nuggets from the Christian scriptures and traditions. I think the scriptures have often been misinterpreted in a way that puts wrong burdens on those who have suffered most and that has been one motivation for me to write the book.

In the first section I suggest that a significant part of forgiving is about separating ourselves from the people who have harmed us. So, in the first chapter I try to unpack what we mean when we say we forgive each other. In the second I look at the idea of stages in forgiving and ask: does it help if I get even a bit of the way on this journey? The third chapter will look at some of the blocks – the things that keep me stuck. The fourth looks at victimhood and asks: do I have to be a victim forever because I suffered some terrible wrong? The fifth looks at how we can move towards letting go of the past.

In the second part of the book I look at Christian forgiving and discuss ways in which it includes but also moves beyond separation. The second chapter in this section asks how God responds to wrongdoers. The third asks how God responds to us when we suffer wrong and find it hard to get rid of our anger.

CHAPTER ONE

Forgiving, or letting go of the past?

When people talk about 'forgiveness' the word can cover at least three things which need to be distinguished:

1. The person wronged forgives.
2. The person who did the wrong accepts forgiveness.
3. Both are reconciled.

What I am talking about here is only one of these: the person wronged forgives. One reason why it is important to distinguish the three senses of forgiveness is that if – and that is a very big *if* – you have been seriously wronged and you decide to move in the direction of forgiving, you need to be sure that you are not burdening yourself with other things – such as the wrongdoer's repentance, or the task of being reconciled with the wrongdoer, both of which are separate. So it is important to work out what you are taking on – and what you are *not* taking on.

This matters because we can have hidden assumptions that we have to do all sorts of things, when in fact many of these things may have nothing to do with forgiving. So one reason for asking what is involved in forgiving is to limit the burden on those who decide to move in that direction, rather than increasing it.

ONE PIVOTAL ISSUE

One pivotal issue is that forgiving is only an issue if a person or group has done something wrong to someone. Before we look at what is involved in forgiving we have to ask some apparently simple questions.

1. Who did wrong?
2. What was the wrong?
3. To whom did they do it?

Before we can address any of these we have to be able to distinguish right and wrong. Some people argue that we cannot do this, because our subjective experience colours our judgement. They are correct in pointing to our biases, which are normally greater than we think. But it makes no sense to conclude that we cannot know right from wrong. Nor is it sensible to argue that just because an individual or a group evaluate an action differently from us, we cannot come to a firm conclusion. Take rape or child abuse: there are people who defend both. That does not alter the fact that both rape and child abuse are wrong, and seriously wrong.

If your loved one has been murdered you know the wrong that was done; and you know it was done to you. You may not know who did it.

There are other cases in which the answers may not be so obvious. Think of family rows, where people have not been speaking for years: can anyone really remember why it started? You might be able to name one person but sometimes other family members were involved directly or indirectly.

Or take the example of single people, especially women. Many have been left with responsibility for their elderly parents just because they never married. There is an unspoken assumption among their brothers and sisters – and often their parents – that single people, especially women, unlike married people with families, have no important responsibilities in their life and should therefore take on more responsibility for the parents than the rest of the family. Their brothers and sisters then combine with the parents to put pressure on the single person. This can cause huge resentment and deep hurt to the single person, which can be worse if unspoken. Is there something to be forgiven? If so, who has done what wrong to whom? The answer may not be that obvious: a series of misunderstandings and assumptions can lead to a confusing situation in terms of right and wrong. Also, looking at it in terms of right and wrong may not be the best way out of the mess.

Another example is the conflict in Northern Ireland. Why did the Troubles start? Many think they know the answer. But if you start to probe, things can get very unclear.

Suppose you cannot really say who did what wrong to whom, does the question of forgiving still come up? I think not. Other things come up, such as what can I do about my resentment, anger, powerlessness, etc. But I can only forgive if I have someone to forgive. And that can only happen if the person has done some wrong to me. If not, then forgiving is not an issue.

Let's assume that we have established who did what wrong to whom. What then do I have to do if I have been wronged and I decide to forgive? Because there is confusion about the answer, and because people often assume that forgiving someone may minimise, excuse or justify a bad act, it is important to try and tie down what we mean by forgiving.

I think there are several elements in it. Two are:

1. To recognise my anger and accept it as legitimate
2. To let go of the desire for revenge by separating myself from the wrongdoer.

ELEMENT 1: RECOGNISE AND ACCEPT MY ANGER

If I have been hurt badly I will be angry. This can cause me fear because I may be afraid that I will not be able to control my anger. I may also feel guilty if I have been taught that I should not feel angry. What am I supposed to do with these feelings? There seems no room to express them in external society: there people expect me to be polite, not filled with fury or guilt. People do not like to hear talk of anger and revenge. They prefer gentleness and mildness. But if I have been hurt badly, I do not *feel* gentle or mild.

Am I not entitled to my anger? Am I not entitled to feel like looking for revenge? Desiring revenge is a natural reaction: I want the persons who wronged me to know what the pain feels like, to give them a dose of their own medicine so that they understand what they did. It is a primitive but normal response. In a society that does not want to deal with anger I have to find some way to express my anger, and I need a way for society and my family to accept that my anger is natural, understandable and appropriate. Without that, what options do I have except to turn the anger on to myself, which can lead to depression, or to project it on to others, which will lead to other problems?

None of the above means that seeking revenge is morally right but simply that desire for revenge needs to be acknowledged and accepted as normal and appropriate.

ELEMENT 2: SEPARATE MYSELF FROM THE WRONGDOER

When I am angry and seek revenge, the wrongdoer is in my head. I think of him or her morning, noon and night – especially at night. Forgiving in part means getting him or her out of my head. That means separating myself mentally from him or her. That means doing something about revenge. Instead of denying that I want revenge, I move, however slowly, towards giving up the desire for it. It means slowly letting go of the past and not being dominated by it. This is a task that I can only do for myself, but I may also be helped by others.

If you agree that forgiving includes at least these steps then it is blindingly obvious that it is very difficult for most people.

CHAPTER TWO

Stages in letting go of the past

One way to look at forgiving is to consider it in terms of stages. This can be useful, provided – and it is an important proviso – some things are kept in mind:

Stages are only an image, a way of looking at things. The assumption in this image is that forgiving is a series of tasks and normally one goes before the other. So people will usually come to terms with their anger and then slowly move away from the desire for revenge.

'Stages' as an image should not be taken literally. No one starts at stage one, finishes it and then moves on to stage two, etc. People are not like that. If the 'stages' image works at all, then people move back and forward continuously through different stages. Some people seem not to go through stages like these at all, but arrive amazingly quickly at complete forgiving.

It can be hard for us to see if we are moving at all from one stage to another, however fitfully. But think of the tide going out: if you are standing up to your waist in the middle of it, the tide may be going out, but that is not what you think when a new wave hits you and goes in quite a bit further than the last. But if you are standing on a headland looking down on the sea you can see soon enough that, despite some waves coming in further than the last, the reality is that it is going out. This simply reinforces the point that a 'stage' is not something that one completes and then mechanically moves on to the next.

Using stages as an image has the danger of bringing in the idea of 'Brownie points': you get them for each stage completed. We can do this either consciously or unconsciously. You might find yourself in a situation where other people who suffered trauma graciously explain to you how they can remember once being at your stage, but fortunately now they have moved on. The thing to do with people like that is to remove yourself from them as far and as fast as you can.

With these caveats there may be some value in thinking of stages as part of moving toward forgiving.

Olga Botcharova[1] worked with conflict victims in the former Yugoslavia. One can imagine some of the horrors involved. There were villages in which mixed ethnic groups lived together with tolerance and respect, many in mixed marriages. Within 18 months of the start of the war many were gang raping other villagers. How does a society, how do the individuals involved, both those wronged and the perpetrators, deal with that?

She suggests that those who choose to move towards forgiving go through the following stages. The same pattern may also apply to people who have suffered from abuse, or loss through violence.

STAGE 1: DENIAL

The first is to deny the experience: it could not have happened. Everything is a daze. Often in the case of a murder people remember little about the funeral, except that there were many people there, expressing sympathy. Sometimes the victim experiences it as a film reel, something she is looking on at, but not part of. Denial can also be an early response to childhood abuse, or to domestic violence. In the first case this is because abuse can be such an attack on our whole sense of personhood that the only response for a long time may be to block it out. In the second it can hap-

---

1. Paper at Woodstock Theological Center, Washington, Colloquium on 'Forgiveness in Conflict Resolution', 9 December 1996.

pen because partners invest so much in their relationship that they need to see the other partner as good, decent and upright, not as a violent thug.

STAGE 2: REALITY

Then reality begins to sink in: he or she is not coming back. The silence will continue. The chair remains empty or the beatings and abuse continue.

STAGE 3: SUPPRESS THE GRIEF

The first reaction to this may be to try to suppress the grief, or to say that you will cope with the abuse or violence. But it doesn't work. The tears flow. For some, the tears never flow. Then, to an extent the grief is repressed. That leads to other psychological problems.

STAGE 4: ANGER

After this comes the anger. Why me? is a common question.

STAGE 5: SEEKING PUNISHMENT AND REVENGE

With the anger comes the desire for revenge. You can be tempted to operate on the thesis that if the wrongdoer is punished then you will be restored to your former position. But of course this will not happen because the experience of losing a loved one through murder, or being abused, or being in a violent relationship changes you. You can never go back to the way you were before.

STAGE 6: MYTHS

You may try to create myths to help you justify revenge, because revenge can be so attractive. These myths can be true or untrue. The original context is kept simple. Olga Botcharova suggests one:

The story is told in terms of heroes and villains: This myth looks especially attractive because the natural instinct of others is to offer sympathy and support to the victim and to punish the perpetrator. But you may pay a price if you focus on yourself as a victim, as we will see below. At a political level it might come out as great powers attacking smaller ones, or the emphasis might be put on breaches of human rights by the enemy.

Some other myths may be ideas about struggle, suffering, or blaming, among other things.

Struggle: 'Struggle' was a big word for Republicans during the Northern Ireland Troubles. So if one of their members was murdered, or killed on 'active service' as they saw it, he or she was killed in the 'struggle' for Irish freedom. That gave the death meaning which made it easier for some to cope. But like the next myth, it helped prolong the conflict.

Service: Unionists interpreted their deaths within the idea of 'service': serving the cause of freedom or democracy, or 'fighting terrorists.' Each year on Remembrance Sunday (around the time of the anniversary of the ending of World War I in 1918) their dead are remembered as part of the war dead in the United Kingdom as a whole. Yet this countrywide liturgy makes it easier for the UK armed forces to get more recruits for the next war.

Blaming: Blaming can be a theme for the wider society, especially the tabloid press who thrive on seeing things in terms of 'good' and 'bad' guys. Murder and abuse is interpreted within this wider framework. It is especially attractive because it highlights the wrong done. It appeals to the need for self-righteousness in us. But does it help us to get rid of the fire in our belly?

Secondly, blaming encourages revenge and thereby can help the person wronged to feel justified in responding to the oppression. This then leads to a cycle of violence.

STAGE 7: A CYCLE OF VIOLENCE

Myths can be attractive – and as mentioned already they may be true or false. But if they end up encouraging us to seek revenge, then there is simply a cycle of violence in which more people suffer and more people do wrong.

Looking at forgiving in stages, with the caveats mentioned at the beginning of this section, can be helpful, but what are some of the things which make it difficult for us to move forward?

CHAPTER THREE

Blocks to moving forward

WRONG ASSUMPTIONS ABOUT WHAT IT MEANS TO FORGIVE

Many people who have been deeply hurt get angry at talk of forgiving. Sometimes this is because they have wrong assumptions about what it involves. If forgiving meant what they think it means, then they are quite right to reject it. So it is worth looking at what forgiving is *not*. I think the following assumptions about it are incorrect:

Wrong assumption A: Forgiving abolishes punishment
Many think forgiving means letting the perpetrator off punishment and so they will not forgive.

In fact it does no such thing.

Let's take an example: Edel and Jim are married. Jim has severely beaten Edel. Edel eventually decides to forgive him, but the police hear about the case and charge him with assault. Should Edel give evidence against him?

My answer is normally 'Yes', if she can cope with this. (We need to be careful about making statements that apply to all situations.)

But how can she do this if she has forgiven him? Does forgiving someone not mean we should oppose the person being punished?

No, it does not. Forgiving a wife-beater means also hoping that he will realise the terrible wrong that he has done, that he will be sorry, that he will try to make recompense, that he will take measures to ensure that it never happens again, such as attending an anger-management course – not mere promises, that he will accept appropriate punishment. One process that may help this is the criminal justice system – it is one of the reasons why it exists. Edel can forgive him, wish him well, then take him to court to ensure he is appropriately punished, and hope that this will encourage him to make the changes in his life that are needed.

Forgiving Jim does not alter the fact that he should be punished for his crime. Nor does it change the duty that the state has to act to prosecute criminals and to punish them appropriately.

In the above case, whether Edel forgave Jim or not he should still have faced the issue of punishment for his crime. (How he should be punished is another question.)

Sometimes the fact that the person wronged forgives the wrongdoer helps the wrongdoer to come to his or her senses. At other times it does not. But even when it does, the issue of punishment remains to be addressed.

Wrong assumption B: Forgiving accepts wrongdoing
No, it doesn't. Let's take another example:

Joanne's husband was murdered beside her in bed one night during the Troubles in Northern Ireland. After many years she was able – slowly and painfully – to move towards forgiving. Does that make the murder any less terrible? Does it excuse it in any way? Of course not. This is because forgiving is something the person wronged does. The stages he or she goes through change him or her. They do not change others, although they can contribute to change. So, if we forgive people we are not letting them off the hook.

Wrong Assumption C: Forgiving is against separation
This is a temptation often faced by some Christians. They know Our Lord forgives us and wants us to be united with him and with each other both in this life and the next. The scriptures tell us again and again that we cannot be united to God unless we try to make peace with each other. Many

therefore assume that forgiving must involve a new relationship with the wrongdoer. But they feel sick at the thought of this because what they really want is to hurt the wrongdoer, not to have a new relationship with him or her. Some married people also feel guilty when they separate from their partner, even an abusive one, because they know some of the scriptural passages about forgiving – and they have forgotten other passages which nuance these.

Other Christians have the opposite temptation: to focus on separation only, and forget that there are other aspects of Our Lord's message.

I will say more later about the Christian view of forgiving. For the moment let me say that if the stages I outlined above mean anything then they start with accepting our anger and desire for revenge and moving on to giving up that desire. That means getting the wrongdoers out of our head. That means separation, often physical as well as psychological. It means that we can live our life without being dominated by them or by the terrible suffering they imposed on us. It means discovering a new autonomy for ourselves. It means that we no longer define our identity in relation to the wrongdoers or the event – though the event remains of great importance in our life.

If I decide to move towards giving up ideas of revenge, what am I doing? For the most part I am letting go of fantasies that I can never fulfil. Even if I could fulfil them they would not satisfy me: suppose I really killed the person who had wronged me, what then? I would still have the bitterness in my belly. The wrongdoer is dead. Am I going to resurrect him and kill him again? What will I have achieved by killing him?

Yet the assumption can be widespread that revenge can help. Look at debates in the US about capital punishment: one of the arguments is that those wronged can get 'closure' once the wrongdoer has been executed. It's a crazy idea.

The real issue is that when I am consumed with ideas of revenge, the wrongdoer is in my head – right bang in the centre of it. I think of him or her often during the day. I wake up during the night thinking about him or her. He or she is the first thing I think of in the morning. This harms me, not the wrongdoer:

- It is my guts that are in a knot, not his or hers
- It is me who is sleeping badly, not him or her
- It is my blood pressure that is up, and my body that suffers all the other physical damage brought on by unresolved trauma, not his or hers.

So the only person suffering from this is me, not the wrongdoer.

If I move away from revenge, I move away from keeping the wrongdoer in my head. I move towards freeing myself from him or her. I move towards separation.

Take the example I used above. Suppose Edel got to the stage where she no longer wanted revenge for what Jim did to her; suppose she left him and started a new life in which he did not figure; suppose she no longer feared him, and no longer thought about him day and night: now she is free. She has separated herself from him. She is no longer focused on destroying him. She is focused on living her own life.

Something else happens in this process: Edel discovers her own autonomy, her own personhood. It is precisely this which has been violated by Jim's violence. By getting Jim out of her head she has a chance of getting in touch with who she is as a person.

There can be a false notion of autonomy, one that suggests that we are all isolated individuals. That is not what I mean. A person is always a person in community. But once we have been violated in a serious way we cannot go back to what we were before we suffered the wrong. We need to create a new sense of ourselves as persons in community, and in a community that is healthier than our old community. Getting Jim out of her head is part of the process by which Edel is able to do this.

Getting to the freedom of separation is the first really important step in forgiving. It may or may not lead on to other steps. But either way it leads the person wronged towards freedom. If other stages on the road to forgiving are to be possible, normally this separation is the first step.

Having said that, separation is not easy. Take the example of Sheila. She was bullied in work by Tim, who was the head of her department. For four years Sheila complained to various authorities without any result. Tim was charismatic and clever. He was more interested in the organisation and his position than in any individual case. To be seen to co-operate with the staff he brought in a consultant to look at the work in the department. The consultant, who knows who writes her cheque, co-operated with Tim, and all her proposals suited Tim. Tim continued to show no sign of having done anything wrong. Sheila ended up hurt, angry and resentful and hates Tim for his wrongdoing and hypocrisy, and also because he continues to be held in high esteem in the organisation.

Mental or physical separation is not easy, because Sheila cannot get another job. So her only choices are to separate mentally from Tim or to continue to have him in her head. Is it possible to separate mentally? Yes, but it is difficult. She can adopt a purely professional manner, objectify Tim in her mind, avoid eye contact with him, work at reducing the number of times she thinks about him during the day. She will not be able to do any of these perfectly, but if she starts doing some of them, she may be surprised, not at her failures, but at the increasing autonomy she begins to discover in herself when she succeeds. She may begin to realise again that she is a person, and that her being a person does not depend on Tim's existence.

This may not sound much like forgiving, but in fact it is

often one of the necessary steps. However, forgiving is also about more than separation, as we shall see.

SELF-RIGHTEOUSNESS

Our capacity to fool ourselves is immense, so we need always to remind ourselves that what we think is wrong may not be wrong at all; or there may be many legitimate reasons why the person we think is a wrongdoer sees the conflict differently from us. Most important of all, we have no reason to feel morally superior to any person in the world, unless we ourselves are without fault.

COMPARING OURSELVES TO OTHERS

Some people forgive overnight, or so it seems. Gordon Wilson is an example. His daughter Marie, a 20-year-old nurse was murdered in the Enniskillen bomb in Northern Ireland on 8 November 1987. He was injured and caught in the rubble. He was able to hold her hand as she died. Her last words were: 'Daddy, I love you.' In a radio interview he said:

> I bear no ill will, I bear no grudge. She was a great wee lassie, she loved her profession. She was a pet and she's dead. She's in heaven, and we'll meet again. Don't ask me please for a purpose. I don't have a purpose. I don't have an answer, but I know there has to be a plan. If I didn't think that, I would commit suicide. It's part of a greater plan, and God is good. And we shall meet again.

He said he forgave her killers and added: 'I shall pray for those people tonight and every night.'

A lot of people were furious with him. They did not want to forgive the IRA. They thought his forgiving let the IRA off the hook. They thought that he was letting down the Protestant community in Northern Ireland. They wanted to hang all in the IRA.

Gordon Wilson suffered because of these attacks. Later,

he made contact with the IRA, asked them why they had done it and tried to persuade them to give up their campaign. He failed.

A different reaction from people who have suffered wrong to Gordon Wilson's story was: 'He is holy. I could never do what he did. So I am not holy.' Underneath that often lies a feeling of guilt: 'I cannot do what I should do.'

In fact the story is a good example of what I mean by forgiving: Gordon Wilson gave up all desire for revenge, he began to ask himself what drove the IRA to do what they did, he worked at understanding their context, he reached out to them and he tried to persuade them to give up their campaign of murder.

He did not make excuses for them. He did not minimise what they had done. He did not justify their actions. He did not say they should go unpunished.

It is not surprising that some other people who have been wronged feel morally inferior because they cannot do what Gordon Wilson did. But they forget one simple point: they are not Gordon Wilson. Each person is different. Each person needs to go his or her own road and make his or her own decisions, at his or her own pace and in his or her own time. Trying to go at someone else's pace will harm us.

Take an example: could I run a marathon today? Not a chance. Could I run a marathon in six months time? Possibly. I say 'possibly' because I know my capacity for good intentions and bad delivery.

Could I climb Mount Everest? Not in a million years. But if I was able to do so I would have to set up a base camp. From there I would head on to the next camp. I would not go straight up. I would often have to go down in order to be able to climb further. I would not be able to do it on my own. I would need teams of people with me. Climbing Mount Everest is difficult. But it may be easier than moving towards forgiving.

So why do we compare ourselves to others? Gordon

Wilson was not married to our loved one. His circumstances and background are completely different from ours. At the same time, a story like his, if heard properly, can be an encouragement: if he went the road of forgiving, who knows what we might be able to do in time – if we want to.

COMPARING OURSELVES TO OUR LORD

Another trap, for Christians, is to compare ourselves to Our Lord: he did it, so why can't we? One answer is because we are not Our Lord!

Yes, we are called to follow Our Lord. Yes, he did say 'Be perfect as my heavenly Father is perfect.' But nowhere in the gospels does it say that we have to achieve this overnight.

We have to be patient with ourselves. One old, old trap is to set ourselves a goal, e.g. giving up drink, then beat ourselves up for not achieving it, and then because we are fed up on account of this we go back on the drink!

It can be the same with forgiving: we can set ourselves impossible goals, and then when we fail we give up the whole idea.

SOCIAL ASSUMPTIONS ABOUT FORGIVING

There are two widespread assumptions about forgiving: that we are all supposed to forgive, and that forgiving lets people off punishment.

I told a friend of mine recently that I was writing something on forgiving and that part of it was dealing with the guilt that was dumped on people. She registered interest immediately, smiled, and asked: 'Is it a sin not to forgive?'

It's a good question. She had put her finger on one social assumption in a Christian country that is often dumped on people who are wronged: you are supposed to forgive. But this is tied to one understanding about forgiving: it is about reaching the final stage, with no mention of in-between steps; or else it is tied to reconciliation, where you and the person who wronged you are supposed to be in a new relationship.

Have you ever been put under pressure to forgive? Have you ever been given a lecture about how wrong it is to hold on to bitterness? Have people dumped the example of Our Lord on you? Has that made you more angry than you were before? Up to this you were angry, and possibly bitter, but now you know – or so they tell you – that you are a bad person.

I am not dismissing Christian forgiving. It is very important, as we shall see below. But it is also complicated and it is often used by people who have not been badly wronged to make those affected by wrong-doing feel bad and guilty.

It is worth noting who makes calls like: 'We must all forgive', 'We all have to move towards reconciliation', 'This is no way for a family to behave.' Have the speakers been deeply and wrongly hurt? Or are they people who have not suffered much but who call on others to do something they do not have to do themselves? If so, they are asking the most vulnerable of all to take on a heavy burden. I think I have done this myself in the past in well-meaning efforts to work for peace. For that I am sorry. Those who have suffered least need to be careful about calling on others to forgive.

This tendency can be very predominant in families and/or in Catholic religious communities. For example, John had a very bad relationship with his brother Gerry. But his other brother Michael had a good relationship with Gerry. So Michael pressurised John to make peace.

What is wrong with that? Are Christians not called to make peace with each other?

There may be several things wrong with it. First Michael is 'triangulating' the problem. He is coming in as a mediator between his two brothers, without being invited to do so. He is taking sides. He is also assuming that he knows John's experience. But he does not. He does not have the relationship with Gerry that John has. So he may not be able to make judgements about who is right or wrong. Usually, but not always, third party interventions like this within family rows make things worse, not better.

A second wrong assumption is that we must punish and, since forgiving means letting people off punishment, we should not forgive. I believe that there is a need for punishment. But when does a desire for punishment become a desire for revenge? Secondly, as already pointed out, I do not believe that forgiving means letting people off punishment.

GUILT

People who find they have problems forgiving can suffer terrible guilt. But is this appropriate or neurotic guilt? Guilty feelings are appropriate when we have deliberately done something wrong to hurt another, not otherwise.

A religious sister I know, Mary, lived in a small community when a new sister called Angela joined. The two did not get on. Yet they were both people who had dedicated their lives to the gospel which calls us all to love one another, especially our enemies. There is no room in this for not getting on with people – or so many think, quite incorrectly. When I suggested to Mary that she might think of moving to another community she said she could not do this because to do so would be a failure in love. So she stayed. In her terms she 'failed in love'. Then, not surprisingly, she got sick.

This is a case in which the issue of forgiving does not arise. Neither of the sisters had wronged the other. Forgiving only arises when someone has done something wrong to someone else. In this case the sisters could not stand each other – a simple, ordinary case of a personality clash. Had they been part of a larger community they might have been able to negotiate greater space from each other than in the small community. So their choices were to learn how to live with each other in a way that they found tolerable, or for one or both to leave the community, or, thirdly, to get sick. Mary chose to stay, she felt guilty, so she got sick because her guilt feelings were inappropriate: she had done nothing wrong.

I think it would have been better if each of them, and her religious superior, had been able to recognise that there was a personality clash, that neither of them was to blame for this, and that it was entirely appropriate for them to live in different places. There are many people I know for whom I have great respect, but I would not like to live with them, nor they with me, and I do not see that as a reflection on either of us.

This is particularly important in religious communities. It is also important in families where conflict between individuals is often not recognised or accepted. As a result family members can be expected to sit together for the sake of appearances at family functions, for example weddings, even though they cannot stand each other, and the other family members know this. The same thing can happen at Christmas because of a false notion that bad relationships can be papered over because it is that time of year. It is interesting that society seems to find it easier to accept marital breakdown than it does breakdown in relationships between brothers and sisters. This may account for some of the heavy drinking we sometimes see at family gatherings, followed by anger and hurt coming out in inappropriate ways.

This is not to say that we can simply walk away from relationships when there are problems, on the grounds of personality clashes. It depends on the type of relationships involved, the commitments made, the responsibilities we have. But personality issues should be recognised in all relationships, and if they were, there might be less hurt.

Many people have unfair burdens put on them by people who have no relationship with them and do not understand what they are going through.

Finally, all who have been wronged can legitimately see themselves as victims and encourage others to do the same. But there are both advantages and disadvantages in doing this and in the next section we will look at some of these.

CHAPTER FOUR

Will I be a victim forever?

In this chapter I want to look at some new emphases which are being given to the status of victimhood. Some people who have been wronged feel that they are benefitting from this, but I want to suggest that a price is being paid for it, and that the price can be high: the fire in their belly can continue to burn.

NEW PROMINENCE GIVEN TO VICTIMHOOD

If I have been hurt by someone one response is to think of myself as a victim.

A friend of mine works in economically deprived areas. She came from a deprived background herself. When she was young she would always try to hide where she came from because she was ashamed of her poverty. Now kids in the areas where she works shout at her that they live in a poor area. The change is significant: poverty is now not something to be ashamed of. Nor should it be. It can give status. It can also help local community activists get funding if an area is recognised by the government as being deprived.

In the media it is easier than in the past to get attention if one is a victim. People are asked to tell their stories. Normally the suffering provokes natural sympathy in listeners. Victims often may not feel this, because they may feel they do not get enough attention, but there is much more focus on the suffering of victims than was the case in the past.

Conferences on social issues often make time for those

suffering from the issue to tell their story. People organising a campaign against drink driving will often look for a relative of a victim to tell the story in public, or else the campaign will be organised by someone who has been bereaved by a drunk driver.

In the past there was more emphasis on a stiff upper lip, on getting on with your life. I have noticed a change especially among Protestants in Northern Ireland. They used to complain that Nationalists were always moaning. The stiff-upper-lip culture was strong among them: it was important not to break down in public. Recently that has begun to change. They have started talking in public about their suffering during the Troubles. They are saying that they were victims too, which often was the reality.

SUPPORT

There has been a growth in the number of victims' groups which offer support to those most affected, and campaign for services on their behalf. In 2007 there were about 150 victims' groups in Northern Ireland. People who have suffered get support from others who have experienced trauma like their own. When support groups organise social occasions it is easier to go out with people who have been through something similar than going to a social occasion where others wonder what to say to you – or at least that's what you think they are thinking. In a victims' group you realise that others have suffered as well as yourself, and some even more. Support groups can also lobby for the needs of victims: working to get benefits, state compensation, training courses. Or they can lobby on an issue: tougher laws on drunk drivers, or looking for enquiries to tell the truth about what happened to loved ones.

VICTIMS AND JUSTICE

Many victims want justice because they want to see the perpetrator punished. But they also want to see themselves vindicated. Vindication has to do with defending oneself, explaining one's position, getting people to accept that you are right and that what the perpetrator did was wrong. It is particularly important in cases of child abuse and rape, because victims who have no reason to do so often take some guilt on themselves. The purpose of the criminal justice system is in part to vindicate them, to punish perpetrators and thereby to encourage public order.

It is obvious that many times victims do not get justice. How many rape victims have brought cases to court and lost, because of insufficient evidence, or because the perpetrator had a better lawyer, or because the jury did not believe them?

A young girl, Sandra, was sexually abused by her father from the age of five until she was 14. When she was 19 she fell in love with a boy, but she became re-traumatised when they tried to have sex. She received counselling and decided to report her father to the police for his abuse. She was encouraged to do this but was also told that once she reported the case she would have no control over the outcome. The file was sent to the Director of Public Prosecutions. A year and a half later she was informed that the DPP was not pursuing the case as there was not sufficient evidence to prove the case beyond a reasonable doubt.

She was devastated. She had reported the crime because she wanted to place the wrong done on the perpetrator and to free herself from carrying some of the guilt. She wanted public vindication – to be told that she was the victim, not a wrongdoer. She also wanted justice. Now the state had let her down. How was she to deal with this? Why should she forgive? How can she forgive?

Part of the answer is that she should not forgive if she misunderstands what forgiving involves – such as thinking that forgiving minimises the wrong, justifies it, or excuses the wrongdoer from punishment.

How many other victims of abuse have been unable to bring cases against their assailants because they were too traumatised to tell anyone what they had suffered? How many victims of the IRA, how many Republicans murdered by security force members, have never seen anyone brought to trial, or if they were, how many had to suffer as those who murdered their loved ones were released early from prison? The reality is that many victims will never get justice.

What can people do, if they have suffered wrong and cannot get justice? For some the answer will be that they want to hold on to the fire in their belly and to continue to seek justice, even though they know it is not achievable. For them it is better to do this than to admit defeat. Admitting defeat, as they see it, will do two things:

1. It will let the wrongdoer off the hook: he or she will not be named and shamed
2. It will face them with something perhaps more painful than chasing after unachievable justice: the fire in their belly which will not go out. At least the chase after justice will allow some distraction from this.

But the fire in their belly will continue to burn, and that will be painful. The wrongdoers will often still not face prosecution.

VICTIMS, TRUTH AND RECONCILIATION

The South African Truth and Reconciliation Commission (TRC) believed that truth could lead to reconciliation. The idea was that if wrongdoers told the truth and those who were wronged heard the truth about what happened to their loved ones, they could be reconciled. The Commission gave a voice to those who were wronged. This was seen as important because one of the things said by torturers during the apartheid regime to those in prison was: 'You can scream all you want. No one will hear you.'

The Truth and Reconciliation Commission was the public symbol which proved this statement wrong.

People still argue as to whether the TRC was a good thing or not. Telling their story did not help all victims: for some it re-ignited the original trauma. In one province of South Africa at the time there were only two psychologists. So when people had finished their day at the TRC no professional support was available for most.

Secondly, the Commission was hoping that victims would forgive. Winnie Mandela (wife of Nelson) was questioned for a week about the murder of 14-year-old Stompie Seipei who had been seized by her bodyguards and was later found dead. One bodyguard gave evidence that he had killed Stompie 'like a goat' with a pair of garden shears. Winnie denied this. Her blanket claims of innocence prompted another truth commissioner, Yasmin Sooka, to describe her testimony as 'particularly painful'.

Archbishop Tutu, Chair of the TRC, at the end of her testimony begged Winnie to admit that 'something had gone wrong':

> I speak to you as someone who loves you very, very deeply, who loves your family very deeply. There are people who want to embrace you. There are many who want to do so, if you were able to say 'something went wrong' ... and say, 'I'm sorry, I'm sorry, for my part in what went wrong.'[2]

Winnie then apologised to Joyce Seipei, the mother of Stompie.

Following allegations of harassment of Stompie's mother by supporters of Winnie during a break in the hearings, Archbishop Tutu called Joyce Seipei to the front of the hall where she embraced and kissed Winnie. Jerry Richardson, who had been convicted of the killing and said he did it on Winnie's orders, stood alongside them.

2. http://www.doj.gov.za/trc/media/1997/9712/s971204v.htm

The 'reconciliation' was rejected by another victim's legal representatives:

How can there be reconciliation unless there is some acknowledgement of the violence that has been committed?' asked one advocate, who asked not to be named for professional reasons. 'People want to know what has happened to their families. They live with the pain of not knowing. Reconciliation is all very well, but now there is at least some doubt as to whether Madikizela-Mandela [Winnie] is telling the truth or not. I think the moment chosen for this reconciliation, when she was not answering questions satisfactorily, was completely inappropriate.

Also unimpressed by thoughts of reconciliation was Caroline Sono, mother of missing Soweto youth Lolo Sono, who demanded that Winnie tell her what had happened to her son Lolo. In an emotional outburst outside the hearing, Sono screamed: 'She's the woman who murdered our children. I will not rest until I find my son's remains. I want Lolo.'

My sympathy is with those who do not see this incident as an example of reconciliation. It seems more like manipulation of a vulnerable victim. Did Winnie tell the truth? Even if she did and if her apology was genuine, what was her apology for? For 'things going wrong'. The issue was the murder of Joyce Seipei's 14-year-old son. Was Winnie responsible for the murder or not? Or was she only responsible for 'things going wrong'?

Even if these questions could be answered, people who are wronged cannot forgive according to a press schedule. Maybe Joyce Seipie wanted to move in that direction. If so she should not have been put under pressure to do so in public in front of television cameras having just sat through a long session on the murder of her son. To me this is an example of dumping moral demands on people who have been wronged – in this case for wider political aims, which in themselves may be desirable.

This incident is a classic example of the confusion which exists around reconciliation and forgiveness. This is the main reason why I have consistently used the term 'forgiving' – which can only be done by a victim – and not 'forgiveness', which is a vague term that points to things both victim and perpetrator can do (in 'forgiveness' the perpetrator receives forgiving).

The fact is that many victims will never find out the truth about what happened to their loved ones. Some will not even learn who the wrongdoers were. Michael Lapsley, a South African whose hands were blown off in a letter bomb – probably sent by the security forces – is often asked if he has forgiven the perpetrators. His answer is:

> I haven't forgiven anyone, because I have no one to forgive. No one was charged with this crime, and so for me forgiveness is still an abstract concept … So my attitude to the perpetrator is this: I'll forgive them, but since I'll never get my hands back, and will therefore always need someone to help me, they should pay that person's wages. Not as a condition of forgiveness, but as part of reparation and restitution.[3]

Further, there is no logical reason why finding the truth should lead to reconciliation. Many people who have been wronged say all they want is to know the truth, not punishment. This may be true, but others who find the truth may then want to focus their vengeance on those they now know were responsible.

Some of the reasons people who have been wronged pursue the truth is so that others will know the horror of what they have gone through, so that wrongdoers will be named and shamed, so that if people are so appalled at

3. http://www.doj.gov.za/trc/media/1997/9712/s971204v.htm

what happened such things will never happen again. These are important aims and the people with the most passion for them are likely to be those who have suffered most. Yet the dilemma is that focusing on these aims keeps people focused on the past. That stirs up anger and the person who has been wronged suffers from that. Some people I know have made a deliberate decision not to seek the truth or justice because they know the harm they themselves will suffer from anger if they focus on the past. Others have said that they were so focused on the wrongdoers that they were unable to grieve.

VICTIMS AND WRONGDOERS

Because of its political advantages wrongdoers sometimes claim to be victims on dubious grounds. So, some paramilitaries who have murdered people, or child abusers, or violent 'ordinary' criminals, or drunk drivers, claim to be victims. And maybe they are: many abusers were themselves abused. Many paramilitaries got involved because they saw a relative or friend murdered. Alcoholism is a destructive disease, so is the alcoholic responsible when he or she gets behind the wheel of a car?

A simple but important distinction needs to be made, and failing to make it leads to all sorts of complications: people who do wrong are wrongdoers. The people they hurt are the persons wronged. There may and often will be suffering in the life of the wrongdoer and because of this he or she may also be a victim. But the distinction is that when he or she faces the person they wronged then, in that context, he or she is a wrongdoer, not a person wronged. In that context she or he did the wrong, the other person did not. The person wronged cannot be blamed for the wrongdoer's suffering in other contexts. Nor can his or her suffering be minimised because of the past suffering of the wrongdoer. Where the past suffering of the wrongdoer may be relevant is in deciding his or her level of responsibility, or the appropriate punishment. There are many cases where things are not as simple as having an innocent person wronged and a guilty wrongdoer. Many conflicts involve wrong on both sides.

But, remember where we started with our definition of forgiving: the first point was that the question of forgiving only arises when a wrong has been done by someone against another person. If nothing wrong has been done there is nothing to forgive. There are plenty of conflicts where it is not clear who has done what wrong and to whom. In those cases the way to make progress towards easing the conflict may not be through forgiving, because the issue of forgiving may not arise at all.

It is clear from all I have said about victimhood that it is important for many people to see themselves, and to be seen, as victims. But is there a price to be paid for this?

THE PRICE OF VICTIMHOOD

Victimhood and identity: To my mind you are a victim if someone has seriously wronged you. But do you want always to think of yourself as a victim, to describe yourself as one, to become one inside yourself?

A victim, according to *The Concise Oxford Dictionary*, is a 'person or thing injured or destroyed in seeking to attain an object'.[4]

This refers to someone who is powerless, someone to whom something is done, for example children abused by adults. They did nothing wrong. Something terrible was done to them.

So, are victims powerless?

To me the answer is yes, in so far as they see themselves as victims. But I immediately add that all victims have the capacity to move towards being survivors. Survivors come out of a bad situation. They remain alive, they carry on, they learn to cope.

---

4. Oxford University Press, 1976.

The paradox for victims' groups is that by definition they exist to help victims. They work to support them and lobby for their needs. But to the extent that they describe themselves and their members as victims they can encourage them to remain victims. The way we describe ourselves influences what we become.

A question I ask victims' groups – as distinct from individual victims – is: to what extent have your members moved from being victims to becoming survivors in the past five years? How many members have moved out of the group because they no longer see themselves as victims? Again, the Brownie point issue comes up: 'good' victims move, 'bad' victims do not. But if the group do not ask this question it is certainly possible, and perhaps even likely, that members are reinforcing each other's victimhood instead of helping each other move to become survivors.

Part of the issue here is how central you see being a victim is to your identity. If someone asks you what you are, how do you respond? That you are:

- A victim?
- A man or woman?
- A husband, wife, partner?
- A mother, father, brother, sister?
- A sports person, worker, young, middle-aged or senior citizen?
- Other?

If being a victim is part of your identity, how central is it? For some it becomes the overriding identity. It is hard to avoid this, because trauma can be so overwhelming. But moving to being a survivor in part means getting back in touch with other central aspects of our identity, however long this takes, and however slow the progress. Some people eventually move to the stage where they are able to say something like: 'I used to say that I was someone whose son was murdered. Now I say that I am a mother, a woman, a community activist, middle-aged, and that the most awful experience I went through was having my son murdered.' That is very different from saying only: 'I was someone whose son was murdered.'

Moving away from making victimhood central to our identity does not mean changing our history. It does not mean forgetting our loved one. It does not mean air-brushing events out of our history. But it means accepting that the terrible injustice I suffered is not the only thing in my life. The world around me has changed since that terrible event. I have changed. And, for the Christian, my loved one who has been murdered has also changed by entering into eternal life with God.

An important challenge in counselling and spiritual direction is to know when to offer support and comfort to a person who has suffered wrong, and when to gently introduce difficult challenges. Doing this too early can be destructive because the person is not ready for it. Yet, not doing it all can lead to collusion in helping a person to remain a victim.

A cycle of violence: Making your central identity that of a victim can also lead to a cycle of violence. If you see yourself as a victim it is hard not to look for revenge. Or else, even implicitly, you can encourage people to take revenge on your behalf, because every time they see you, they may think of the wrong done to you. This is particularly the case if the attack on you is seen as an attack on the wider community, as will happen in civil conflict. But what happens, if you, or others on your behalf, seek revenge? Those you hurt will look for revenge in response and a cycle of violence develops. They get hurt, you get hurt, and so it goes on, from generation to generation. Do you really want this?

The above comments are about social blocks to forgiving. But what can you do at a personal level to move towards it, if you want to do so?

CHAPTER FIVE

Letting go?

How can we move towards letting go of the past? If I could give you a nice, simple answer to the question of how to let go of the past you would know I was lying, because there isn't one. Also, what helps one person may not help another. Having said that, here are some ideas that may help.

FOCUS ON YOUR OWN FREEDOM, NOT ON FORGIVING

Maybe you have been trying too hard to forgive. Or maybe you have been trying to do something you do not believe in. Or perhaps you have been told to do something that you do not want to do. You may feel pressurised by others to do it. So, stop trying to forgive! You might be trying to do something that is not forgiving at all. But try something else: try to get yourself some freedom. Freedom from what? Freedom from being dominated by the person who hurt you; and freedom from those who continue to condemn you.

After all, who is suffering because you keep thinking about the wrongdoer? Whose guts are in a knot? Who is not sleeping at night? Who is tormented every moment of every day? It may be you, not your enemy.

The trouble is that all our different feelings can be mixed up like threads in a ball of twine. So the hatred I feel for the wrongdoer is mixed in with the terrible pain I feel about losing my loved one, hatred of myself for having feelings of hatred, confusion as to why this has happened to me. So the easiest thing is either to express my anger or repress it.

But suppose I could be free of him or her; suppose my every moment was not taken up with him or her; suppose I discovered a new sense of freedom; suppose I could live a life not dominated by him or her – would that not be great?

FILTER THOUGHTS

Try not to think of your enemy. At times this will be impossible. Even if you succeed in keeping him or her out of your head for a while he or she will come back, so the effort seems useless.

Yet it depends in part on how realistic you are in your expectations. If you hope to expel someone from your mind completely and immediately, then the situation is hopeless. Few can do that. But if you set out to reduce gradually the number of times you think about the wrongdoer, and you encourage yourself every time you succeed rather than blaming yourself for the times you fail, then things may change slowly.

BE GENTLE WITH YOURSELF

Encouraging yourself is part of this. So also is trying to laugh at your failures! That may seem absolutely impossible, but I have seen people do it. Laughter puts things in perspective. It recognises our limitations, but also our possibilities. It gives encouragement. Is it such a big deal if you fail? Are you a statue, or a human being with flesh and blood? If the latter, you cannot perform according to a programme or schedule.

Laughter also gives us the idea that failure – and if you are trying to get trauma out of your head you will fail – is not the end of the world.

PRAY

Pray for freedom. Do not look for an answer overnight. In my own experience, if I get into a row with someone, praying seems at first completely useless. But after a period this seems less true. Sometimes, looking back on times I prayed about a row, I can see that the prayer was not hopeless as it then seemed, and that Our Lord, as he promised, was in fact walking alongside me, leading me gently in the direction of life.

Don't let yourself get into a guilt trip in prayer. We will be looking at some faith reflections shortly. One basic message from these is: Yes, Our Lord cares deeply for wrongdoers, but he is also deeply angry with them. And it would be crazy if we ended up with the idea that he cares for wrongdoers, but rejects you because you are not yet a perfect saint, and have not yet reached the fullness of forgiving.

GET SUPPORT

Don't give into temptations to close your door and isolate yourself. It is hard not to do this. Look for support from friends, family, clergy, or counsellors. But choose wisely: do not choose people who are going to look down on you, or who make impossible moral demands, or who listen for a while but then tire of your moaning. Also do not look only for those who just support you, but never challenge you. If you do this, you will be like the victim of a car accident whose legs were badly injured: he looked for, and got, a nice, gentle physiotherapist who made no demands on him, who did not push him to walk even with the pain. So a year later he still could not walk.

We need people who can sense what is going on in us with empathy, who care for us and who are committed. But we also need people who, at the right time, can raise difficult and challenging questions for us to face. We do not need people who reinforce our victimhood.

HONOUR YOUR LOVED ONE

If your loved one has been murdered, honour his or her life. Every time you think of the murderer, you take the focus off your loved one. Honour the life of your loved one by living: living is for this life, not the next.

Honouring your loved one means accepting his or her life as good. That means accepting the death as part of his or her life. It's not the time or the way of death that you would have wanted for him or her, but it is what happened. Somehow accepting this is part of accepting our loved one's life as it was, not as we wanted it to be.

This also involves letting our loved one go. There is a paradox here: the more we try to hold on to someone who has gone, the more we stop ourselves from living here and now, and instead live in the past. We freeze our loved one's life at the moment of death, whereas for the believer in God life goes on after death. For those who do not believe in God, focusing on the death alone does not do justice to the full life of our loved one. That can involve implicitly denying the meaning there is in the whole of life.

Paradoxically, the more we can let our loved one 'go', the more we accept their life as it was. We define their life, not by their death, but by their whole life, of which their death was part. We focus on the goodness that we have been given through him or her, rather than on the harm done them by the wrongdoer. We focus on our loved one, not on the wrongdoer.

HONOUR YOURSELF

If your conflict is because of a bad relationship, you may need to accept that some relationships cannot be repaired. Sometimes we have to live with separation, not as a step towards a new relationship, but as the end of one. That is life. It can sometimes do more harm than good to try to keep relationships going because sometimes the hurt and guilt continue with them. This does not mean that we have to think badly of the other person: we can wish them well, but accept that we will not have a relationship in the future.

Take the following two examples:

> a) Jean got married young and two years later the marriage broke up. She returned home. She never saw or met her husband again. Eventually she got on with her life and re-married happily.
>
> b) Her sister Betty fell out with their brother who had abused her when they were young, but her parents did not believe her. She continued to see her brother regularly for the rest of her life because that was expected by the family. As a result her trauma continued.

In one case there was physical separation, which helped, but not in the other. This is an example of harm being done by attempting to keep a relationship going.

In part this means accepting the limitations of ourselves, of others and of life. Perhaps the most important message in the area of forgiving is that we are called to do our best, no more and no less.

The same point comes up if you have been abused: here it is often incredibly difficult to honour yourself, because abuse by its very nature tears at the centre of who we are. So again do the best you can to honour yourself, but be gentle with yourself when you fail.

TRY TO SEE THE EVENT IN A WIDER CONTEXT

I know of some people who have coped with the murder of a loved one, or abuse, through seeing the event in a wider context.

Sabine Dardenne was 12 when she was kidnapped and sexually abused by Marc Dutroux in Belgium. She coped in part by recognising that bad things happen in the world, and that it was her bad luck to be caught by an abuser. It is a factual view: there has never been a period in history without some humans causing other people pain. This helped her to avoid guilt about her abuse – many abuse victims feel irrational guilt. It also helped her to take a more balanced view of the future. Shortly after her rescue she wanted to go out on her bike. Her mother was horrified, because she had been on her bike when Dutroux kidnapped her. But Sabine replied that it was hardly likely that he would escape from prison, come back to the same place and kidnap her again. Her mother's reaction was understandable, but Sabine's reaction was realistic.

Other people have been able to find meaning in a terrible event or conflict as part of the plan of God. It is a view that leaves me uneasy because it can suggest God is a sky pilot playing with all of us as puppets. But it can also be a way of accepting that God is greater than all the evil in the world, and that in the end God's desire for goodness for all of us will triumph.

ACCEPT THAT CONTEXT MATTERS

We are all much more influenced by our context than we realise. So we may do things in one context which we would consider truly bizarre in another.

Take parents at a football match in which their young children are playing: they often become extremely angry at the referee's decision because their young Johnny is – in their view – not being treated fairly. They may have absolutely no interest in football and know nothing about it, but they may come close to murder in those circumstances. In another context, the same people will be mature, gentle, considerate, balanced and willing to look at different points of view.

I know paramilitaries who during the Northern Ireland conflict fully supported the idea of killing policemen in front of their children. Now some of them say to me: 'What was all that about?' They now wonder how they ended up killing people. But they were only able to ask that question long after the violence had ended. While the violence was on-going, killing policemen seemed to them an obvious thing to do.

In a conflict situation, especially a family one, we can get ourselves into a corner and say or do things that we would not have said or done in a different context. As the years pass we change. So does our context. So if you feel bitter against someone remember that you have changed, and so also have they. Whatever the row was about in the past may not be relevant now.

There is a story told of a German ex-soldier who approached Jean Monnet, one of the original group who influenced the start of the EEC (now the European Union). The soldier said that he wanted to work with Monnet on the project. However, he wanted Monnet to know some things about his past before he decided whether or not to accept him. He told Monnet that he had been in the German army, that he had supported his country's war aims, and that he had been one of the troops who had occupied Paris. Further, he was not apologising for any of this. Monnet, a Frenchman, considered his response for a moment and then said: 'If you believe in our ideals for the future and want to commit yourself to them, then you are welcome to join us.'

The two men disagreed deeply about the past, but they had common aims for the future. On that basis they were able to go forward together. No guilt was admitted, no remorse expressed, no forgiving offered. Yet they managed to work together.

Sometimes something similar can work in our relationships. That does not mean changing our moral evaluation of what happened in the past, but it does mean accepting that others see things differently, that the context has now changed, and whatever about the past, we can work together for the future.

In my view this is not forgiving. But that does not lessen its value.

As I said at the beginning of this section, these are simply ideas that may help some people. What matters is that you find some way to respond that slowly eases the extent to which your life is dominated by the loss or conflict you have endured.

In the next section I am going to look at some texts from the Bible and ask what issues they raise for Christians who have been deeply and wrongly hurt. What can we learn about how God sees us when we are hurt, angry and tempted by revenge? Is the Bible a burden or a help to us when we have been deeply wronged?

PART TWO

God, separation and moving beyond it

CHAPTER SIX

Christian forgiving

Everything we say about God can only give us a glimmer of what God is like, because God is a mystery. So we can only speak in images and analogies. In the above discussion I have mainly focused on two elements involved in forgiving:

1. Recognising and accepting my anger.
2. Separating myself from the wrongdoer.

However, in Christian forgiving there are two additional elements. The first two that we have discussed are difficult but these are even harder:

3. Developing a degree of empathy with the wrongdoer by distinguishing between the bad act and the person who did it.
4. Wishing the wrongdoer well.

EMPATHY IN CHRISTIAN FORGIVING

I have emphasised the place of anger, the need to recognise and not repress it, the appropriateness of it not only in those who have suffered terrible wrongs, but also in others who care for them, or care about justice and right relationships, or care about the good of society as a whole.

Yet now I want to raise a different question, one that can only be raised with most people who have been wronged after they have experienced deep anger, after they have touched the overwhelming fire inside themselves, after they have been tempted to and fantasised about multiple revenge, and after they have slowly and painfully separated themselves from the wrongdoer and given up on notions of revenge.

Empathy is moving in the opposite direction from separation. In separation we get the wrongdoer out of our head. In empathy we begin to allow thoughts about him or her to re-enter, but from a completely different starting point.

When we first separate ourselves from the wrongdoer we are getting something out of our head that has a certain unreality about it: a view of the wrongdoer that is focused only on the wrong he or she has done. The reality is that there is always more to people, no matter who they are, than the wrong they have done. They are also husbands, wives, mothers, fathers, sons, daughters, sports people, workers, readers, etc. In many of these roles they may act in good and caring ways.

Empathy means realising that those who do wrong should not be defined only by their action: there is more to them than the bad act that they did. They may have other parts of their life where they are really good. Of course that does not excuse or minimise or justify the harm that they did. For the person wronged it means beginning to think of the perpetrator in a more rounded way: trying to separate the person from the person's behaviour; loving the sinner but not the sin.

Is there a limit to empathy? Can one have empathy with a child abuser or Nazi, or Josef Fritzl? Again, the answer is clearly 'No' – if you think empathy has something to do with excusing, minimising or justifying wrong. But if you see empathy as an attempt to step inside the world of the wrongdoers to try to understand why they did what they did, then maybe it is possible.

This, for most people, is really difficult. It may show why people's natural reaction to the question: 'Should we forgive Josef Fritzl?' is entirely understandable. Who in their right mind could think of having empathy for such a person? Yet the New Testament is clear that Our Lord tries to have empathy with every person, no matter what he or she has done.

WISHING THE WRONGDOER WELL

This again does not mean excusing what they have done, or letting them off punishment. But it can mean things like hoping that they will change their life, repent of the wrong they did and move into a better, more human space.

This for me is the final stage in forgiving. Many see it as impossible because they are afraid that it will minimise, excuse or justify the wrong. Or else they think it means letting people off punishment. It has nothing to do with any of this, as we have seen in Chapter Three.

Wishing someone well is the other end of the spectrum from trying to destroy him or her through revenge. It can only be done by someone who has received the gift of freedom – and freedom is a gift. Forgiving is only possible in the context of this gift.

If you reach this stage and the wrongdoers do not respond but remain stuck in their view that what they did was right, this is not your problem. You have completed your journey towards forgiving. You have no responsibility for their response. That is their business. The fact that you offer forgiveness may help them to repent. But they may also reject it.

So, in a family situation, it may be that you have taken all the steps that lie in your power to forgive your parents or brothers and sisters for some wrong that they did to you. This is where you need to accept that you have nothing more to do.

EACH ELEMENT IN CHRISTIAN FORGIVING IS IMPORTANT

Whatever you think about them, each element in Christian forgiving is important. That is why it is both wrong and dangerous when people make a statement like: 'Forgiving means wishing the wrongdoer well.' It does not. Part – and only part – of forgiving involves that. But another, equally important, part is recognising the appropriateness of our anger. A further part is separating ourselves from wrongdoers by getting them out of our heads. If we say forgiving is any one of these, instead of saying that each of them is part of forgiving, then we either dump a moral task on the persons wronged ('You must forgive, but I do not want to hear about your anger') or we tempt them to stay stuck in one part of forgiving ('Hold on to your desire for revenge'). I see both strategies carried out in the name of Our Lord and that grieves me, because I am convinced it adds greatly to the pain and trauma of those grievously wronged.

I want now to look at some scriptural passages that illustrate some of the themes on which we have touched.

CHAPTER SEVEN

God and the wrongdoer

GOD'S ANGER

One of the good aspects of much modern Christian theology is that it has stressed the idea of God's forgiveness and mercy. This is a balance to the past when the focus was on an angry God. However, there is a real danger that in making this necessary adjustment we lose sight of the fact that sin makes God angry. We can end up trivialising wrongdoing. That is not the emphasis that we see in the scriptures. God's anger is mentioned over one thousand times in them.

Take some of the sayings of Amos, a prophet who lived about 750 years before Our Lord. He tells those who have trampled on the poor:

> Therefore, because you trample on the poor
> and take from them levies of grain,
> you have built houses of hewn stone,
> but you shall not live in them;
> you have planted pleasant vineyards,
> but you shall not drink their wine.
> For I know how many are your transgressions,
> and how great are your sins –
> you who afflict the righteous, who take a bribe,
> and push aside the needy in the gate. (Amos 5:11-12)

Anyone who thinks the scriptures are old hat, and not really relevant to today, should read that passage, especially in the light of the corruption exposed in politics in Ireland in the past five to ten years, and the murders by paramilitaries and some security force members in Northern Ireland, and child abuse by clergy. Amos is showing God is angry because God's children are being hurt by other people.

In the Old Testament God is often seen as a judge. In our context a judge decides on right and wrong in a court. But in the Old Testament God as judge is seen as making things right. He not only makes a judgement on who has been treated badly and who was responsible; he also changes the situation to a more just one:

> Can wicked rulers be allied with you,
> those who contrive mischief by statute?
> They band together against the life of the righteous,
> and condemn the innocent to death.
> But the Lord has become my stronghold,
> and my God the rock of my refuge.
> He will repay them for their iniquity
> and wipe them out for their wickedness;
> the Lord our God will wipe them out.
> (Psalm 94:20-23)

In the New Testament we often see Jesus being angry. Look at the story of him clearing the Temple, where he found people selling cattle, sheep and doves, and money changers:

> Making a whip of cords, he drove all of them out of the temple, both the sheep and the cattle. He also poured out the coins of the money-changers and overturned their tables. He told those who were selling the doves, 'Take these things out of here! Stop making my Father's house a marketplace!'
> (John 2:15-16)

We are also told that the anger of God will descend on those who lead children astray:

> If any of you put a stumbling-block before one of

> these little ones who believe in me, it would be better for you if a great millstone were fastened around your neck and you were drowned in the depth of the sea. (Matthew 18:6)

Who is the anger of Jesus directed against? It is directed against those who do wrong. But given the way that some talk about reconciliation, you might think that Our Lord's anger was directed against those who cannot forgive. So, according to this scenario, Jesus takes the offender, offers him or her forgiveness, holds him or her to his breast as a shepherd holds his lamb, and then throws the person who has been wronged out of the house.

That makes no sense.

You might respond, 'Look at the story of the unjust servant':

> For this reason the kingdom of heaven may be compared to a king who wished to settle accounts with his slaves. When he began the reckoning, one who owed him ten thousand talents was brought to him; and, as he could not pay, his lord ordered him to be sold, together with his wife and children and all his possessions, and payment to be made. So the slave fell on his knees before him, saying, 'Have patience with me, and I will pay you everything.' And out of pity for him, the lord of that slave released him and forgave him the debt. But that same slave, as he went out, came upon one of his fellow-slaves who owed him a hundred denarii; and seizing him by the throat, he said, 'Pay what you owe.' Then his fellow-slave fell down and pleaded with him, 'Have patience with me, and I will pay you.' But he refused; then he went and threw him into prison until he should pay the debt. When his fellow-slaves saw what had happened, they were greatly distressed, and they went and reported to their lord all that had taken place.

Then his lord summoned him and said to him, 'You wicked slave! I forgave you all that debt because you pleaded with me. Should you not have had mercy on your fellow-slave, as I had mercy on you?' And in anger his lord handed him over to be tortured until he should pay his entire debt. So my heavenly Father will also do to every one of you, if you do not forgive your brother [or sister] from your heart. (Matthew, 18:23-35)

His master forgives him an enormous debt. Then he goes and locks up one of the other servants who owes him a tiny amount by comparison. The master is furious and punishes him for failing to respond to others the way the master had responded to him.

The point is that we are all sinners. We have all been forgiven by God. So we should forgive others the wrong they do to us.

This is a major emphasis of Jesus' teaching. But is there not a difference between someone who is filled with thoughts of revenge because her husband has been murdered, but who does not act on these thoughts, and the servant in the story who really hurt his fellow servants for a minor offence? The point is not that forgiving is unimportant, but that we need to face the fact that it is a difficult task for anyone who has suffered terrible abuse, and who is rightly angry as a result, to move towards forgiving. God will not beat us up just because we cannot achieve this instantaneously.

Separation between God and the Wrongdoer

There are many different ways to handle conflict. We have seen above that if we are to get a wrongdoer out of our head we have to separate ourselves mentally and sometimes physically – when that is possible from him or her.

Read the following story:

So Abram went up from Egypt, he and his wife and all that he had, and Lot with him, into the Negeb.

Now Abram was very rich in livestock, in silver, and in gold. He journeyed on by stages from the Negeb as far as Bethel, to the place where his tent had been at the beginning, between Bethel and Ai, to the place where he had made an altar at the first; and there Abram called on the name of the Lord. Now Lot, who went with Abram, also had flocks and herds and tents, so that the land could not support both of them living together; for their possessions were so great that they could not live together, and there was strife between the herders of Abram's livestock and the herders of Lot's livestock. At that time the Canaanites and the Perizzites lived in the land.

Then Abram said to Lot, 'Let there be no strife between you and me, and between your herders and my herders; for we are kindred. Is not the whole land before you? Separate yourself from me. If you take the left hand, then I will go to the right; or if you take the right hand, then I will go to the left.' Lot looked about him, and saw that the plain of the Jordan was well watered everywhere like the garden of the Lord, like the land of Egypt, in the direction of Zoar; this was before the Lord had destroyed Sodom and Gomorrah. So Lot chose for himself all the plain of the Jordan, and Lot journeyed eastwards; thus they separated from each other. Abram settled in the land of Canaan, while Lot settled among the cities of the Plain and moved his tent as far as Sodom.' (Genesis 13:1-12)

The story shows one way to handle conflict. It is not rocket science. It's called separation. The problem was simple and as old as human beings: shortage of resources led to conflict. Abraham's answer is separation. That solved the problem, at least for a while. So, if someone tells you that there is no Christian basis for separation, talk to them about Abraham and Lot in Genesis Chapter 13.

Jesus also talked about separation. This was in the context of good people being separated from those who did wrong. Look also at the following passage:

> The Pharisees came up and started a discussion with him; they demanded of him a sign from heaven, to put him to the test. And with a profound sigh he said, 'Why does this generation demand a sign? In truth I tell you, no sign will be given to this generation.' And, leaving them again, he re-embarked and went away to the other side. (Mark 8:11-13)

Jesus walked away from them.

There is also the instance when Jesus and his disciples were rejected by the Samaritans. Samaritans and Jews were traditional enemies:

> As the time drew near for him to be taken up, he resolutely turned his face towards Jerusalem and sent messengers ahead of him. These set out, and they went into a Samaritan village to make preparations for him, but the people would not receive him because he was making for Jerusalem. Seeing this, the disciples James and John said, 'Lord, do you want us to call down fire from heaven to burn them up?' But he turned and rebuked them and they went on to another village.' (Luke: 9:51-56)

Again, he walked away. Was he reconciled with the Samaritans? Not in this instance. He had tried to build a relationship with them and they had refused. So he moved on.

Finally, look at the instructions Jesus gives his disciples when he sends them out on a mission:

> Whatever house you enter, stay there, and leave

> from there. Wherever they do not welcome you, as you are leaving that town shake the dust off your feet as a testimony against them. (Luke: 9:4-5)

Separation, of course, is not the end of the story, because God never gives up on us. Jesus will come back to the sinner. Also, the New Testament shows us that Jesus learned through being challenged by others that the Good News was not only for his own Jewish people, but for others, including Samaritans, who were their enemies. But to say that separation is not part of the story is untrue. It is. So, a person who is wronged and decides to separate herself or himself from the wrongdoer is not doing something unchristian. She or he is doing something which is part of the journey towards reconciliation illustrated by Our Lord himself.

Separation can be physical or mental or both. It is only one way to handle conflict. It is not always an option, but if it is available, do not dismiss it on the grounds that it is anti-Christian.

GOD PUNISHES

Why was Jesus so angry at the sellers in the Temple? As a Jew he would have offered sacrifice in the Temple and seen it as an important institution in his faith. But he also modified the central role of the Temple for Jews by introducing a new centre of faith: himself as the Son of God. The real problem was that the sellers had turned the Temple into a marketplace. To some extent this was not surprising. The Old Testament stressed the need for sacrifice and that this should be done on behalf of the people by the members of the priestly tribe of Levites. These were not supposed to work, but to be supported by the people. That led to corruption, which impacted especially on the poor. This was being done in the very place in which sacrifice was being offered to his father.

So did Jesus say: 'I forgive you'? Did he minimise or justify or excuse what the sellers were doing? No, he got a whip and used it left and right. He turned over their money tables. He roared with prophetic and righteous indignation at their abuse. He drove them out of the temple.

We can also see the anger of Jesus towards the Pharisees throughout the gospels. Why? Because they were putting terrible burdens on other people's shoulders which they themselves did not have to bear. This was in the context of terrible poverty. The Pharisees were educated. They knew the law. So they could keep it. The poor did not. So they could not keep it. That made the Pharisees holy and the poor unholy. It really angered Jesus that they were telling people that his father would not love the poor.

In the parable of the Last Judgement the sheep are on his right and the goats on his left. The goats are banished into everlasting fire because 'I was hungry and you gave me no food, I was thirsty and you gave me nothing to drink.' (Matthew 25:42)

THE ANGRY GOD LOVES THE WRONGDOER

We need to be careful with all these sayings of Jesus about anger, separation and punishment: some are the words of the early Jewish members of the church in dispute with their Jewish brothers and sisters who did not follow Christ. Also, the anger of God is one part of God's response to wrongdoing. It is not all of it. God's anger is never vengeful: vengeance seeks the destruction of the other; loving anger seeks to call the wrongdoer back to life. The anger of God is always of this second kind.

Nonetheless, it would be strange if hurting those whom God loves did not cause God anger. So, not only can God understand our anger when others hurt us wrongly, but God shares it. Our anger is not something to be ashamed of. It is not only natural, it is also appropriate. But for God it is not the final word. Nor must it be for us.

People often think anger excludes love. It need not. The fact that God is angry with people who do wrong does not reduce his love from them. The scriptures make this point over and over again.

Jesus weeps over Jerusalem:

> Jerusalem, Jerusalem, the city that kills the prophets and stones those who are sent to it! How often have I desired to gather your children together as a hen gathers her brood under her wings, and you were not willing! See, your house is left to you, desolate. For I tell you, you will not see me again until you say, 'Blessed is the one who comes in the name of the Lord.' (Matthew 23:37-39)

His tears show the pain of a lover who has been unable to get a response from the loved one. But he will not give up on her.

The same theme is shown in the parable of the lost coin in which the woman searches the whole house looking for it and then rejoices greatly when she finds it. (Luke 15:8-10) Above all, the story Jesus tells of the Prodigal Son shows how much God longs to be reunited with sinners:

> There was a man who had two sons. The younger of them said to his father, 'Father, give me the share of the property that will belong to me.' So he divided his property between them. A few days later the younger son gathered all he had and travelled to a distant country, and there he squandered his property in dissolute living. When he had spent everything, a severe famine took place throughout that country, and he began to be in need. So he went and hired himself out to one of the citizens of that country, who sent him to his fields to feed the pigs. He would gladly have filled himself with the pods that the pigs were eating; and no one gave him anything. But when he came to himself he said, 'How many of my

father's hired hands have bread enough and to spare, but here I am dying of hunger! I will get up and go to my father, and I will say to him, "Father, I have sinned against heaven and before you; I am no longer worthy to be called your son; treat me like one of your hired hands".' So he set off and went to his father. But while he was still far off, his father saw him and was filled with compassion; he ran and put his arms around him and kissed him. Then the son said to him, 'Father, I have sinned against heaven and before you; I am no longer worthy to be called your son.' But the father said to his slaves, 'Quickly, bring out a robe – the best one – and put it on him; put a ring on his finger and sandals on his feet. And get the fatted calf and kill it, and let us eat and celebrate; for this son of mine was dead and is alive again; he was lost and is found!' And they began to celebrate.

Now his elder son was in the field; and when he came and approached the house, he heard music and dancing. He called one of the slaves and asked what was going on. He replied, 'Your brother has come, and your father has killed the fatted calf, because he has got him back safe and sound.' Then he became angry and refused to go in. His father came out and began to plead with him. But he answered his father, 'Listen! For all these years I have been working like a slave for you, and I have never disobeyed your command; yet you have never given me even a young goat so that I might celebrate with my friends. But when this son of yours came back, who has devoured your property with prostitutes, you killed the fatted calf for him!' Then the father said to him, 'Son, you are always with me, and all that is mine is yours.' (Luke: 15:11-31)

There are two wrongdoers in this story: the younger

and the older son. The younger son has chosen to break the relationship with the father. The older son resents the father's forgiving the younger. How does God react to them? The younger brother runs out of money, comes to his senses and returns home. The father sees him while he is still a long way off. He races down the road like a young fellow. When the son starts his speech – which is rather long – the father does not hear a word. Instead he leaps on the boy, kisses him, hugs him, dances with joy, and shouts to the servants to get a great feast ready. Then he invites all his friends, brings his lost son up to the top of the table and sits him down in the place of honour.

Does this minimise, excuse or justify the wrong the son has done? No. But it does show how much God wants to forgive.

Meanwhile the older brother who has been out in the fields working, comes back and asks what all the fuss is about. When he hears about the feast in honour of his young brother, he goes completely crazy with anger. Eventually the father goes out to him to persuade him to come in. But the older brother is having none of it: the younger brother has disgraced the family, he has gone off and wasted the family fortune, he has no right any longer to be a member of the family.

The story shows how compassionate God is to sinners. So, if you find you cannot forgive someone and you think this is wrong, remember that God will be compassionate to you as well.

You might be sickened that the younger brother is treated like a lord when he returns. Your sympathy may be with the older brother who would not come into the meal. In response to this, people often make the point that the older brother had separated himself from the family because he was not concerned about the younger brother. That is true. But how does the story end? Where is the father? He is outside with the older brother, understanding what he is going through, showing him compassion, but also inviting him gently to take a difficult step. And the father will stand in solidarity with him until the older brother is able, however slowly, to let go of his desire for revenge.

So God understands our anger. God will not simply throw us out of the feast if we are too angry to take part. God will go outside and stand with us.

During his passion and death Jesus showed the extent to which God will go in his effort to save those who do wrong: he offered forgiveness from the cross. The Creed tells us also that he descended into hell. Hans Urs von Balthasar, a Catholic theologian, has a meditation on Holy Saturday in which he sees Christ, after his death, descending into hell in order to stand beside those who had separated themselves from God, so that although they had separated themselves from God, God, in Christ, would stand beside them.[5] But the separation cannot be overcome from God's side alone. The sinner, by God's grace, has to repent.

The scriptures are a challenge to us when we have been wronged. God is also concerned about the well-being of the wrongdoer because God loves him or her. Even if we remind ourselves of God's anger and the punishment that wrongdoers bring on themselves, it is still very hard to share God's love for someone who has hurt us badly. Yet that is what Our Lord does, and it is to this that God is gently calling us.

None of this minimises, excuses or justifies wrongdoing. In fact, by showing the depth of God's love, it gives us glimpses of how terrible wrongdoing is because of the suffering it causes not only us, but God who is infinitely good.

---

5. 'Mysterium Pascale', in J. Feiner and M. Lohrer (editors), Mysterium Salutis, III/2, Cologne: Einsiedeln, 1970, pages 133-326.

CHAPTER EIGHT

God, us and our anger

VICTIMHOOD AND THE SCRIPTURES

There is a lot about victimhood in the scriptures. As we have seen, in the Old Testament God has deep compassion for those who have been wronged and wants to undo injustice as far as possible. One theme of the Old Testament was that when bad things happened to people it was a sign that God was punishing them for their sins. This idea is still influential: many survivors of the 2004 Asian tsunami said on television that it happened because God was punishing them.

The Book of Job knocks this idea on the head. In the story, Job is seen as a just man, whom God hands over to the power of Satan to see if he will reject God when he suffers misfortune. Job does not. So his suffering was not the result of his sins: he was innocent. The point of the story, however, is that Job responded to his misfortune by continuing to praise God. His central identity was not that of a victim, but of a worshipper of God.

A second theme about suffering is that it is accepted as part of the following of Christ. Jesus asked his followers to 'deny themselves and take up their cross daily and follow me'. (Luke 9:23) As always, though, we have to be careful: this saying is about persecution suffered because people follow Christ. There is plenty of such persecution in the world today, but that is not an argument to accept injustice. For example, it would be utterly wrong to say to someone who suffered child abuse that they should put up with their suffering as a means of identifying with Christ. Such a statement would be an outrage. There are connections one might find between the cross and child abuse, but that is not one of them. So, if the acceptance of suffering is praised in the gospels it is praised as one of the conse- quences of preaching the gospel. Some Christian preach- ing has done great harm by encouraging people to accept injustice in a passive manner.

St Paul often boasts of his suffering. But this boasting is different from someone who sees their main identity as one of victimhood. Paul does not make his central identity that of a victim. His central identity is one of being a per- son who has been saved by Christ. He boasts about his suf- fering, not for its own sake, or because he is going to stay as a victim, but because he sees this suffering as a neces- sary part of his following of Christ. That gives him great joy, not sorrow.

Finally, there is the example of Jesus himself. Surely Jesus' main identity was being a victim? Not so.

Jesus is a victim because he is presented as the sacrifi- cial lamb. When he rises he still bears the marks of the cross – he asks Thomas the apostle to put his hands in his wounds and believe. But the scriptures lend no support to the idea of seeing victimhood as the central identity of Jesus. The cross was not the end. It was the triumph of Jesus because he was faithful to his Father, faithful to what it means to be human, faithful to us, faithful to love. But after the cross came the resurrection. In the resurrection Christ is presented as serene, at peace, one who wishes peace on all his followers. (Read the resurrection accounts and notice how often he wishes people peace.) After the resurrection he ascends to his Father, to be reunited with the Father who had handed him over for us. Then he sends the Holy Spirit who is the love of the Father for the Son and the Son for the Father, and the Holy Spirit brings us peace, hope, courage, fortitude and other gifts.

The cross, then, is followed by the resurrection, the

sending of the Holy Spirit and the call to build a new community of peace and respect in our world today. Christ now is the Risen Christ, not the victim.

If we define ourselves mainly as victims we focus on our own suffering. As we have seen, this is sometimes unavoidable. But to persist in it has costs for the person involved and it is not something supported by the gospels.

DO WE WANT TO BE HEALED?

There is a story in John's gospel where Jesus meets a man who had been ill for 38 years. This was at the pool called Bethesda. Sick people used to lie near it, believing that if they could get to the pool when the water was disturbed they would be cured. Knowing the man had been there for a long time, Jesus asked him: 'Do you want to be made well?' The man's answer is interesting. It was not: 'Of course I want to get well. I am desperate to get well. There is nothing that matters more to me in the whole world.' Instead he said: 'Sir, I have no one to put me into the pool when the water is stirred up; and while I am making my way, someone else steps down ahead of me.' (John 5:6-7) In the story Jesus gives him physical healing. But there is no indication that he got spiritual healing.

That question, 'Do you want to get well?', is a hard one. It stands before anyone involved in a conflict, or who has been abused, or who has lost a loved one through drugs, or drunk driving, or violence. No counsellor, no doctor, not even God can make us well if we do not want it.

It is not easy to want healing, because wanting it involves costs: it can be easier to focus on truth and justice than to face the awful reality that our loved ones are not coming back, that we have to let them go, that we can never change the past, that we may lose our status as a victim. Our stomach may churn at any of these because the cost of change is high. But so also is the cost of remaining ill. So the question remains: do we want to be healed?

GOD INVITES US NOT TO BE SELF-RIGHTEOUS

Many of the sayings about self-righteousness will be familiar to you. One is: 'Why do you see the speck in your neighbour's eye, but do not notice the log in your own eye?' (Matthew 7:3).

We have no basis for being morally superior to anyone else. I may not have killed anyone, but I have done harm. Further, I have received great graces, and I know nothing about the background and life of someone who has killed someone, so I cannot conclude that I am better than someone who has murdered.

There is a danger that people confuse self-righteousness with making judgements about right and wrong: I should not be self-righteous, but I should make judgements about right and wrong. I should condemn wrong actions, but I should never condemn another person. And I should welcome other people condemning my wrongdoing because that way I may learn something about myself that needs to change.

There are a lot of 'shoulds' in that paragraph. Each of them is important. When we leave out one of them, things go wrong.

For example, it would be utterly wrong to say to a person who suffered abuse: 'Judge not and you shall not be judged', if by doing so we are asking them not to condemn the wrong done to them. They should condemn the wrong. In time they may be able to distinguish between the bad act and the person, but only some can get to that stage, and then only slowly.

GOD OFFERS US HEALING

Healing is in some ways a better image for people who have been wronged than forgiving. Forgiving has a lot of moral weight attached to it: we can believe – incorrectly as we have seen – that we are letting the wrongdoer off the hook if we forgive. We can feel depressed at not responding in the way we think Our Lord wants us to when we find we cannot let go of anger.

Healing can be natural. If you cut yourself and you keep the wound clean the chances are that it will heal itself – if it is not too deep. The passage of time can make it easier for some people to deal with trauma. Some can be helped by focusing on healing rather than trying to forgive, because it has less moral weight attached to it. However, this will not be true for others, and they will need professional help.

Praying over the healing stories in the gospels can help. If the Christian message means anything, then the healing stories in the gospels are not just for people 2,000 years ago, they are for us today. That means that they can be of some real, practical use to us. One way of praying that has helped many is to imagine the scene. Read the story of the blind man, Bartimaeus:

> They came to Jericho. As he and his disciples and a large crowd were leaving Jericho, Bartimaeus son of Timaeus, a blind beggar, was sitting by the roadside. When he heard that it was Jesus of Nazareth, he began to shout out and say, 'Jesus, Son of David, have mercy on me!' Many sternly ordered him to be quiet, but he cried out even more loudly, 'Son of David, have mercy on me!' Jesus stood still and said, 'Call him here.' And they called the blind man, saying to him, 'Take heart; get up, he is calling you.' So throwing off his cloak, he sprang up and came to Jesus. Then Jesus said to him, 'What do you want me to do for you?' The blind man said to him, 'My teacher, let me see again.' Jesus said to him, 'Go; your faith has made you well.' Immediately he regained his sight and followed him on the way.' (Mk 10:46-52)

Go over the story in your imagination: see the place and

the people, hear the sounds, smell the different scents. Then watch the story as it unfolds. For instance, hear Bartimaeus crying for help; see the disciples scolding him and telling him to be quiet. Then see the change which comes about in the scene when Jesus calls him. Watch Bartimaeus' face as the disciples tell him to have courage because Jesus is calling him. Watch how he leaps up and throwing off his cloak gets them to lead him. (His cloak would be important to a beggar. But Bartimaeus has simply walked away from it because he is hoping for something infinitely better.) Hear the question that Jesus asks him: 'What do you want me to do for you?' and listen to his answer. (It was given immediately because Bartimaeus knew exactly what he wanted, unlike the man at Bethesda pool): 'Let me see again.' Look at what happens to Bartimaeus next, the change that comes over him, the difference it makes to him that he can see. But note also that Jesus said to him: 'Your faith has made you well' and that Bartimaeus now follows him.

Then go through the story again, but this time with yourself in place of Bartimaeus. Instead of being blind, describe your own suffering. Get in touch with your desperate need for healing. Hear Our Lord coming along the road. Ask him for healing. See what happens next in your imagination.

Note also, that Bartimaeus had not always been blind. He knew what it was like to see. He was desperate to see again. His sight was restored. In conflict situations, especially where a loved one has been killed, we cannot go back to what was there before. But Bartimaeus also did not go back to where he was before: yes, he got his sight back, but he had changed in the meantime; so had the world. Above all, he had changed because he had encountered Jesus. As a result of that he 'followed him on the way.' He was not going back to the past, because nothing would ever be the same again. The miracle of receiving his sight was as nothing compared to the miracle of discovering Jesus.

It is unlikely that you will suddenly feel all the pain easing out of your body when you pray like this. But after your prayer is over, look back on it and note what you have felt. Not much may seem to have happened. But if you keep looking back, sometimes you will notice things that went on which you had not noticed a few weeks before. You may see healing. You could not notice it at the time because healing takes time. It is like the growth of your children: you do not notice it daily, but when they are growing fast you can see it after a few weeks.

THE SCRIPTURES OFFER US FREEDOM

Much of what I said about healing applies also to freedom. As we saw above, Jesus' question to Bartimaeus, 'What do you want?', is an important one, and sometimes not one that can be answered quickly or easily. Do you want freedom? Of course the obvious answer is 'Yes'. But are you sure? Because freedom will change you. You will no longer be a victim. You will be giving up your status as a victim. Do you want this? Spending time on this question and then asking for what you really want can help.

THE SCRIPTURES CALL US TO FORGIVE

Certainly one of the passages you will be most familiar with, and perhaps the one that has caused you most angst when you think of your anger and conflicts, is Jesus telling us to turn the other cheek:

> You have heard that it was said to those of ancient times, 'You shall not murder'; and 'whoever murders shall be liable to judgement.' But I say to you that if you are angry with a brother or sister, you will be liable to judgement; and if you insult a brother or sister, you will be liable to the council; and if you say,

'You fool', you will be liable to the hell of fire'. (Matthew 5:21-22) and,

You have heard that it was said, 'An eye for an eye and a tooth for a tooth.' But I say to you, Do not resist an evildoer. But if anyone strikes you on the right cheek, turn the other also; and if anyone wants to sue you and take your coat, give your cloak as well; and if anyone forces you to go one mile, go also the second mile. (Matthew 5:38-42) and,

But I say to you, Love your enemies and pray for those who persecute you. (Matthew 5:44)

It seems clear that if you are full of anger, hatred and feelings of revenge you can never be a follower of Our Lord. So, to repeat a point from the beginning of this book: not only do you suffer great injustice when someone hurts you wrongly, you now know that you cannot be connected with Our Lord, because if you have all these feelings you cannot do what he asks.

Not only that, you also know that Our Lord colludes with wrongdoers because he opposes all punishment or resistance to them.

Or is there something wrong with this reaction?

One response is that we need to be careful about taking what Jesus says in one place and applying it to all places and times. We also need to avoid trying to dodge the challenge of what he says on the basis that it only applied in his context.

If we make the statements about loving our enemies absolute, what are we going to do with the other statements in which Jesus shows anger, and threatens punishment? Why not make them absolute instead?

We need to ask which gospel sayings we highlight most. Everyone can quote the sayings about enemies. But what about sayings about robbery and other sins? Why are these not given the same prominence?

What does Jesus ask of us in these passages about loving our enemies and what was the context in which he was speaking?

The context was one in which the Roman Empire occupied Palestine. For Jews this meant that their holy places were violated, so they saw the occupation as sacrilege. It also meant that they had to pay taxes to middlemen (themselves Jews, like Matthew the tax collector who became one of the disciples). It was a society in which there was terrible poverty, without any social welfare, and much violence. The poor, with whom Jesus mostly associated, were virtually powerless. Jesus, either because he was a principled pacifist – as many believe – or because he saw the hopelessness of violence, opposed armed resistance. So, how were the people to respond to oppression by Roman soldiers?

One interpretation of the saying, 'If anyone strikes you on the right cheek, turn the other also' is that in the culture of the time a Roman soldier would only use the back of his hand to strike a lowly peasant. If he used his open hand, or his fist, he would be treating the peasant as his equal. If the soldier was right-handed – as most would be – he would hit the peasant on the peasant's right cheek. (Try it – gently! – with someone and you will see what I mean.) If the peasant responded by turning his left cheek, what is the soldier to do? You can't get a decent swipe with the back of your right hand at someone else's left cheek. You either hit him with your open hand, or your fist, and the soldier, for reasons of dignity could not do this. So, by turning the other cheek, the peasant was showing that he was not cowed by the soldier and that he considered himself his equal. He was also making a fool of him, because the onlookers would understand that the soldier could not hit him again with his open hand.

'Making a fool of him': how does that fit with Jesus telling us not to call our brother or sister a fool? There are two answers: the soldier will only continue to appear a fool as long as he keeps trying to hit the peasant on the right cheek with the back of his hand. So turning the other cheek is an encouragement to him to stop and to become more human. Secondly, the saying about 'fools' was addressed to the internal Jewish community.

The same sort of principle can be applied to the saying about the tunic: if someone took your tunic and you gave him your shirt as well, you would be naked. That was a problem for the Jews. But the problem lay with the person who caused the nakedness. So the problem would be that of the soldier. Even if the soldier did not pay attention to Jewish culture he would be in trouble with his superiors for upsetting them.

Again, if the soldier asks you to go one mile, go two: the Romans set their own limits in what they could ask of the local population. So for how many miles is the soldier going to use you to carry his goods? Two, three, four, or five miles? At some point he will have to dismiss you, or he will be in trouble for upsetting the delicate balance that the colonisers wanted to maintain with their subjects.

The point about all this is not the details of the interpretations, but to emphasise that there are different understandings of these sayings. If you are feeling guilty because of your feelings of revenge, why do you immediately pick an interpretation that puts a great burden on yourself, when this may not be what Our Lord is asking of you at this time?

Ah, but this argument does not hold up when we come to the saying about love your enemies. If you have feelings of revenge for your enemy clearly you do not love him, so now we know you are at fault. Or, again, is it that simple?

At one level it is simple: Our Lord does call us to love our enemies. He said this and he showed this love in his own life by the way that he responded to those who were persecuting him. But to repeat a point made earlier: loving someone does not exclude anger at their wrongdoing. It does not minimise or justify wrongdoing. And it does not exclude punishment, which – if it is appropriate – will be good not only for the wrongdoer, but also for society. (The issue of punishment needs another book.)

So, am I called to love my enemy who is the cause of all my suffering? The answer is an emphatic 'Yes'. Further, every time we pray the prayer Jesus taught us, the Our Father, we make a dangerous request: 'Forgive us our trespasses, as we forgive those who trespass against us.' Jesus teaches us to look for the same level of forgiving for ourselves as we offer to others. That is why the Our Father is the most difficult prayer in Christendom.

In the light of this if I refuse absolutely to move towards some of the stages of forgiving I cannot pray the Our Father. It makes no sense. But if I have problems with forgiving, then I can pray it. In effect I am saying something like: 'Lord, I have great problems with your prayer, but I am trying. Please help me. You are better at forgiving than I am, so please try to do better in forgiving me than I have so far in forgiving others. I accept that you want me to keep on trying and I will do so.'

So Our Lord's call to me to forgive is strong. But that call is addressed to me as I am, in my actual situation. I am called to do what I can, no more, no less, with the rider that the love of Christ is always calling us beyond where we are.

Further, on that difficult journey towards loving our enemy, we have a friend in Our Lord, not another enemy throwing even more burdens on us. Because he is our friend he is not going to be shocked or horrified at our feelings of anger or revenge. He will understand these, because he shares our anger and horror at what has been done to us. He will walk with us as we move slowly towards the freedom of no longer being dominated by what has happened to us. Slowly and gently he will then invite us beyond that to think about the situation of the wrongdoer, the lostness within which he or she exists. Finally, he will ask us in time to wish the wrongdoer well, not in a way that minimises, excuses, or justifies the wrong done, but one in which we hope that the wrongdoer will come to his or her senses, repent, turn away from evil action, confess the crime, and seek to make whatever restitution is possible.

THE SCRIPTURES CALL US TO BE RECONCILED

> So when you are offering your gift at the altar, if you remember that your brother or sister has something against you, leave your gift there before the altar and go; first be reconciled to your brother or sister, and then come and offer your gift. Come to terms quickly with your accuser while you are on the way to court with him, or your accuser may hand you over to the judge, and the judge to the guard, and you will be thrown into prison. (Matthew 5:23-25)

During the Troubles in Northern Ireland I often thought that if this saying of Jesus was taken seriously there would be a lot of interruptions in Mass as people went off to be reconciled.

So, there you have it. At the end of this whole discussion we are back to where we started: you have to be reconciled with your enemy, and if you are not reconciled you stand accused and guilty.

Or, again, is it that simple?

This book has been about forgiving, not reconciliation. Forgiving is only one part of reconciliation, the part that lies in the power of the person wronged. The person who has been wronged can do nothing about repenting – that is the task of the wrongdoer. Nor can he or she ensure reconciliation by forgiving. The other side has to take responsibility for its part in reconciliation.

So, if you have been wronged you do not have to ask yourself if you are reconciled. You need to ask if you are doing what you can, no more, no less, to move in the direction of forgiving.

Secondly, many people misread the saying about leaving your gift on the altar. They think it reads: 'If you have anything against your brother or sister ...' But that is not what Jesus says. Instead he says: If 'your brother or sister has something against you ...' So, if you have examined your conscience and find that you have not acted unjustly towards anyone else (remembering that it is easy for us to fool ourselves in this area), then the saying does not apply to you. You may of course come to the altar in the full knowledge that someone blames you for something – wrongdoers often do this. Should you then leave and be reconciled? Not unless you really have done something wrong. The fact that someone thinks you have done wrong does not make this a reality. However, we should ask ourselves carefully, taking account of our natural bias, whether he or she is correct or not in their accusation.

Thirdly, even if you find that you have offended others, pause before you rush off to be reconciled. You are now the wrongdoer – whereas this book has been addressed to the person wronged. If you are the wrongdoer you have to ask: does the other person want to see you? Will your appearance add to his or her trauma? Whose need are you trying to fulfill: your own need to be forgiven, or the needs of the person wronged? Sometimes things are best left alone. It is always a matter of judgement as to whether it is wiser to try to make a relationship better or to accept that there is no obvious way to do so. With that important proviso, as Christians, we are called to do what we can to make relationships better.

Conclusion

It has always struck me that life is very unfair to people who suddenly suffer a catastrophic loss through murder, or drunk driving, or who have suffered from abuse, or the suicide of a loved one, or who are faced with a traumatic family conflict, or other similar trauma. They have often done nothing to deserve this. They see themselves as ordinary people, not as heroes. The loss they suffer is massive. Yet, not only do they have to endure this suffering, they are also faced with the great problem of finding a way to live their life after this event.

I suggested that forgiving involves four elements, each of them important:

1. Recognising my anger and accepting it as legitimate.
2. Letting go of the desire for revenge by separating myself from the wrongdoer.
3. Developing a degree of empathy with the wrongdoer by distinguishing between the bad act and the person who did it.
4. Wishing the perpetrator well.

In fact, achieving any of these means travelling a long distance on a difficult journey. Each, even on its own, is life-giving to the person wronged. So if you have been deeply wronged, think of yourself, of your own health, sanity, freedom and life. Do you want to be tied mentally to the person who hurt you for the rest of your life? Or do you want to move, however slowly and fitfully, towards freedom?

The journey, as I have stressed constantly, is not easy,

which is why I think those who can move in the direction of any of them are heroic.

Above all, we should not see Our Lord as our enemy, standing in judgement over us, as we face this work. We should see him rather as he is presented in the gospels: someone who calls us to move towards forgiving, but who himself is also filled with anger at the wrong done to his brothers and sisters, and who will not minimise, excuse or justify it, and who stands in compassion by our side. At the same time he also loves the wrongdoer and calls him or her to repent.

Look also at the way Our Lord loves us. It is good to think back on the times when we have experienced God in our life as someone compassionate and caring. It may be that getting back in touch with this experience (it will always be new) may help us to find healing. Healing can lead to freedom. And freedom can lead to forgiving, even to Christian forgiving.